Storm Chasers

By
Kathleen Thompson

Illustrated by
Susan Lexa

Columbus, OH

The **McGraw-Hill** Companies

Photo Credits

Cover, Back Cover ©PhotoDisc/Getty Images, Inc.;
22 ©Jon Davies.

SRAonline.com

 SRA

Send all inquiries to:
SRA/McGraw-Hill
8787 Orion Place
Columbus, OH 43240-4027

Printed in the United States of America.

ISBN 0-07-604471-8

2 3 4 5 6 7 8 9 MAL 10 09 08 07 06

Contents

Chapter 1
Crazy Ideas

"Are you crazy?" I heard my dad bellow. His powerful voice boomed out of the kitchen and almost shook our old farmhouse. The cat looked up and then replaced her head on her paws. I just continued to read. Mom and Dad were having a silly talk. I wasn't worried.

They were talking about one of Mom's friends. She wanted to come visit, but Dad seemed to think Mom's friend was strange. He was saying he couldn't be comfortable with Mom's friend in the house, but I could tell he was kidding just a little. That's how my dad is.

"Dolores is my oldest friend," I heard Mom say.

"She's a storm chaser. She chases tornadoes. She's wild!" said Dad.

Mom laughed. "She's also a math teacher," she said. "And her husband is a science teacher."

Dad gave a hugely dramatic sigh. "Why would anyone want to chase a tornado?"

Chase tornadoes? That sounded really different and interesting! We live in Oklahoma, and there are lots of tornadoes in Oklahoma. Usually, though, people don't chase tornadoes—they run from them. Tornadoes are extremely dangerous, and you must be careful with them. I put down my book and went into the kitchen. "What's a storm chaser?" I asked curiously.

"Well," said Mom, "you know about tornadoes in Oklahoma."

"They're very dangerous," said Dad. "They cause a lot of damage."

"Yes, they do," said Mom. "Some people drive around this part of the country looking for tornadoes and other storms. They take helpful photographs and measure the storms," she explained.

"*They* think it's cool," said Dad, sticking out his tongue at Mom. "Normal people don't go after something so dangerous!"

Mom playfully poked Dad's arm. "You're not so normal yourself." Then she looked at me. "My friend is always very careful when she follows storms. She knows what she's doing and always returns unharmed."

I remembered that Dad's brother had once been in a tornado. Was this why Dad was acting so funny? "Uncle Luke was in a tornado, right?" I asked.

Dad's face instantly changed. He became serious, and Mom patted him on the back. "Yes, Rebecca," she said, "your uncle was in a tornado."

"It was really awful," said Mom. "Your uncle Luke and aunt Victoria lost nearly everything. The tornado destroyed the house, the barn, the car, and even the fences. Most of their belongings had to be replaced."

"The weather service issued a warning first, so Uncle Luke and Aunt Victoria went to the basement where it was safe," Dad said.

Chapter 2
Why Chase Storms?

Dad looked out the window at the surrounding fields. Western Oklahoma is incredibly flat, so you can see for miles from our house. "I hate tornadoes," Dad said. "They're dreadful. I don't think people should play with them."

"But the warning saved Uncle Luke," Mom said. "And storm chasers help weather reporters."

"Storm chasers don't just take photographs," said Mom. "They report tornadoes and learn how tornadoes build and rebuild. At least, my friends Dolores and Tony Sanchez do. They help the weather service save lives." Mom smiled at Dad. "You know, some people might say *you're* silly for working outside under the scorching sun all day."

"You're right," Dad said. "Dolores is your friend, so they can visit a while. But all they'll want to talk about is frightful tornadoes!"

"Then maybe you'll learn something," Mom said to Dad, and she winked at me. "I'll call Dolores."

Grown-ups are funny, I thought, and I returned to reading.

Mom telephoned Mrs. Sanchez and started giggling softly. Dad made a funny face at me and walked outside to do some work.

In bed that night, I thought more about storm chasers. It seemed unsafe to me. How could storm chasers safely chase tornadoes? I'd be frightened, but I suppose it would be exciting if I was careful.

Right before I fell asleep, I wondered what Mr. and Mrs. Sanchez would be like. What would they look like? Would they look like normal people? Or would they look different? I couldn't wait to talk to Mom's friends and find out all about storm chasers. Slowly I drifted to sleep.

A week later, the Sanchezes arrived in a small van. Mrs. Sanchez was small and plump, with bright, friendly eyes and a pretty smile. She scampered to our front porch and hugged Mom tightly. "Oh, you look wonderful!" she said, laughing and rehugging Mom. Mom was laughing too. She was happy to see Dolores.

Mr. Sanchez was tall with curly dark hair, glasses, and a shy smile. He walked up to the porch and shook Dad's hand meaningfully and then hugged Mom gently and said hello to me. Dad seemed surprised that the two of them looked so normal. I liked both of them instantly.

Mom walked the Sanchezes upstairs to the guest room, and Dad and I looked at each other as he started to laugh playfully.

"Why are you laughing?" I asked.

"They don't look how I thought they'd look," Dad said. "They look like you and me."

"What did you think they'd look like?" I asked.

He shrugged his shoulders. "I don't know. Like movie heroes or something."

"That's how I thought they might look too," I said. "They seem very friendly."

"Yes, they do," Dad said. "But they still do pretty strange things."

"Maybe there's a reason for that," I said.

"Maybe," he answered, shrugging again.

"Dad, have you ever seen a tornado?" I asked. He nodded. "What was it like?" I asked.

"It moved across the land like a powerful giant."

"A giant?" I asked. All I could imagine were two enormous feet dropping from the clouds.

"A giant," Dad said seriously. "Big and fast and hungry."

Chapter 3
All About Chasers

About an hour later, Dad went to work in the fields, and I went to my friend Rita's house. We played a fun game and then went out to a nearby field to look for old arrowheads. We were unsuccessful, however, and became disinterested. I returned home, where Mom and Mrs. Sanchez were on the porch playing dominoes and laughing.

I sat on the porch and asked Mrs. Sanchez lots of questions.

"How fast do the winds in a tornado blow?"

"The fastest tornado ever recorded had winds spinning at 318 miles per hour," Mrs. Sanchez said, restacking the dominoes. "Your car goes only 60 miles per hour, so 318 is pretty fast."

My eyes opened wide in disbelief.

"How close can you get to a tornado?"

"That depends on the tornado. We've discovered that sometimes we'll see one fifteen miles away, but it'll be sunny and pleasant where we are. If we get too close, it becomes dangerous." I thought about Uncle Luke and Aunt Victoria. That tornado came too close.

"Sometimes one large tornado can disintegrate into lots of smaller tornadoes," Mrs. Sanchez continued. "So we have to be really careful to watch where each tornado is moving. We always call the weather service to tell them when more tornadoes have formed. Then they can issue a tornado warning so other people know."

"Are you really scared when you chase tornadoes?" I asked.

Mrs. Sanchez grinned. "I know some people disapprove, but the reason I chase tornadoes is that they're so powerful and fascinating to watch. Sometimes I get nervous, but we're always very, very careful. If a tornado gets too close, Mr. Sanchez and I know exactly what to do."

"Do you dislike thunderstorms?" she asked me.

I shook my head. "No, I actually really like storms. I like when the rain pours, when the lightning lights and relights the sky, and the way thunder makes the whole house tremble."

"That's a little like why I enjoy watching tornadoes. Nature can be quite amazing," she said.

"Everything we learn is used to help people stay safe," Mrs. Sanchez said. "We tell people when a tornado is forming, we discover where and why tornadoes form, and we find the best ways to stay safe."

I wished Dad had been around to hear all this. I'd tell him later.

The Sanchezes left the next morning, but before they left, they showed me some of their storm-chasing tools in disorder in the back of their van: a laptop computer to get weather reports, radar, a camera, and a cell phone.

"We checked the weather this morning. We're lucky—the weather is perfect for tornadoes," Mr. and Mrs. Sanchez said gleefully.

"Lucky?" said Dad as they drove away. "They think it's lucky?" Then I retold him everything Mrs. Sanchez told me. He listened and was quiet. Then he looked at me and smiled sheepishly. "You know what? I was wrong for disagreeing," he said. "Maybe I was the foolish one!"

I was glad he understood.

Chapter 4
The Warning

At lunch, the radio reported a tornado watch, but it was no big deal because there are lots of tornado watches in Oklahoma in the summer. We're more mindful about tornado warnings. There's a big difference. A watch means a tornado might form, but a warning means there is a tornado.

After lunch, Rita came over, and we played outside. When it started to feel cooler, we returned inside.

Dad came in too. "It looks like a storm out there," he said. "The sky is almost black."

We looked out the window. The sky was getting darker and more discolored, and it was only four o'clock.

Rita and I listened to the radio. "A tornado watch is in effect," the reporter on the radio said. Still there was no tornado warning. The radio wasn't loud. In fact, it was becoming difficult to hear. Suddenly there were powerful noises that sounded like rocks hitting the roof. It was hail.

"I don't like this," Dad said.

"The radio hasn't reported a tornado warning," Mom said.

"I know," Dad said, "but I don't like it."

"Maybe I should go home," Rita said, moving her wheelchair toward the door.

"No," Mom disagreed. "You shouldn't go outside. Stay here. Your parents know you're safe here."

After a few minutes, the hail stopped, and even though it was very quiet, we could hardly hear the radio. We couldn't hear what the disintegrating voices were saying, so Mom turned it off.

"Is the storm over?" I asked.

"Let's just stay inside," said Dad. "It's better to be safe than sorry."

"This could be the calm before the storm," Mom said thoughtfully.

"What's that?" I asked.

"When a tornado is coming, there's a big storm, and then sometimes the storm stops, and it's very quiet. Then the tornado comes."

I looked out the window. The trees weren't moving at all. Was this the calm?

But minutes went by, and no tornado came.

Mom reconsidered. "I guess it's over. Don't you think so, Christopher?"

"I guess so," said Dad, and he got up from his chair. "I'll give you a ride home, Rita."

The two of them moved toward the front door, and then the telephone rang.

I picked up the phone. It was Mrs. Sanchez.

"Don't be afraid, dear," she said. "Just go to the basement."

"Why? What's going on?" I asked.

"It's a tornado," said Mrs. Sanchez. "It's moving toward you."

I turned away from the phone. "It's Mrs. Sanchez," I whispered in disbelief. "A tornado is coming right at us!"

I turned back to the phone and listened carefully.

"We're right in front of the storm," said Mrs. Sanchez. "We're close to your farm, and we'll try to get there, but you and your family must go to the basement now."

I hung up and retold Dad what Mrs. Sanchez had said.

Chapter 5
The Storm

Dad rushed to the basement door. "Come on, girls."

I hurried downstairs, and Dad carried Rita, while Mom quickly grabbed Rita's wheelchair and followed us. Then the cat came down. Dad closed the door, but he thoughtfully didn't lock it because he wanted it to be open for the Sanchezes.

Everything was silent, and then we heard the siren that meant there was a tornado warning. Suddenly the basement door flew open, and Mrs. Sanchez came down the stairs with Mr. Sanchez hurrying after her. Dad slammed the door and locked it. We looked at each other gratefully and sighed with relief.

We heard a noise like a train growing louder and louder. I grabbed Mom, and Rita started to cry, so Mrs. Sanchez hugged Rita.

"Don't worry," Mrs. Sanchez whispered to Rita.

We heard crashing. Suddenly the train noise disappeared, and it was quiet again. We all huddled in the basement, listening nervously.

It was over. Rita stopped crying, and Dad opened the door. We carefully crept up the stairs. Dad said he would be brave and go first. We trailed behind, and Mr. Sanchez carried Rita.

It was light in the house. It was too light. Then I knew—we were looking at the sky!

Oh no! The living room was gone! The roof, the second floor, and two walls had disappeared, and the TV was also gone. Later, we found the TV near the barn, a chair in my tree house, and a table in the garden. We were all very lucky that no one was hurt.

Of course, it was not all just luck: Mr. and Mrs. Sanchez had saved our lives. Dad was the first to say how grateful we were. "Thank you, Dolores," he said to Mrs. Sanchez. He started to say more, but he just hugged her. I think he was crying a little. I was crying too.

"Were you really close to the tornado?" I asked Mr. Sanchez.

"We saw it when it touched the ground, but we were far away, so we were safe," he said. "But then it began to move toward your house, and we were suddenly at a disadvantage. We started driving. It seemed to follow us the entire way."

"We got here just in time," Mrs. Sanchez said. "We called the weather service, and they started the siren."

I was extremely upset about our house but thankful we were okay. I was even a little excited that I had been in a tornado—but not too excited. One tornado was quite enough for me!